50 Low-Carb Korean Favorite Recipes for Home

By: Kelly Johnson

Table of Contents

- Kimchi and Pork Belly Stir-Fry
- Spicy Korean Beef Lettuce Wraps
- Cauliflower Kimchi Fried Rice
- Korean BBQ Chicken Skewers
- Zucchini Noodles with Spicy Pork Sauce
- Korean Egg Roll Wraps
- Tofu Kimchi Soup
- Beef Bulgogi Lettuce Wraps
- Korean-style Beef and Broccoli Stir-Fry
- Spicy Korean Cucumber Salad
- Sesame Ginger Bok Choy Stir-Fry
- Korean Beef and Mushroom Skewers
- Spicy Kimchi Cauliflower "Rice"
- Korean BBQ Tofu Lettuce Wraps
- Kimchi Cauliflower "Fried Rice"
- Stir-Fried Beef and Vegetables
- Korean-style Spicy Grilled Shrimp
- Eggplant Kimchi Stir-Fry
- Korean-style Beef Zucchini Noodles
- Spicy Korean Chicken Drumsticks
- Sesame Cauliflower Rice with Beef
- Korean Beef and Vegetable Stir-Fry
- Spicy Kimchi Tofu Stir-Fry
- Korean-style Cabbage and Beef Stir-Fry
- Low-Carb Kimchi Pancakes
- Spicy Korean Radish Salad
- Korean Beef Lettuce Wraps with Pickled Vegetables
- Tofu and Vegetable Bibimbap Bowls
- Korean-style Cucumber Noodle Salad
- Spicy Korean Pork and Cabbage Stir-Fry
- Korean-style Beef and Pepper Skewers
- Cauliflower Kimchi "Fried Rice"
- Spicy Korean Beef and Cabbage Stir-Fry
- Korean-style Sesame Green Beans
- Low-Carb Korean BBQ Beef Bowls

- Spicy Kimchi Chicken Stir-Fry
- Korean Beef and Spinach Stir-Fry
- Spicy Tofu Kimchi Soup
- Korean-style Stir-Fried Shrimp and Vegetables
- Low-Carb Kimchi Fried Cauliflower Rice
- Korean-style Spicy Cabbage Salad
- Cauliflower Kimchi Stir-Fry
- Korean Beef and Bean Sprout Stir-Fry
- Spicy Korean Chicken and Vegetable Skewers
- Korean-style Sesame Spinach Salad
- Low-Carb Kimchi Cauliflower Rice Bowls
- Spicy Korean Tofu and Mushroom Stir-Fry
- Korean Beef and Bell Pepper Stir-Fry
- Kimchi Cauliflower "Fried Rice" Bowls
- Korean-style Spicy Zucchini Noodles

Kimchi and Pork Belly Stir-Fry

Ingredients:

- 1 lb (450g) pork belly, thinly sliced
- 1 cup kimchi, chopped
- 2 tablespoons gochujang (Korean chili paste)
- 2 tablespoons soy sauce
- 1 tablespoon sesame oil
- 1 tablespoon rice vinegar
- 2 cloves garlic, minced
- 1 teaspoon ginger, minced
- 1 onion, thinly sliced
- 2 green onions, chopped (for garnish)
- Sesame seeds (for garnish)
- Cooking oil

Instructions:

Heat a large skillet or wok over medium-high heat. Add a drizzle of cooking oil.
Add the thinly sliced pork belly to the skillet and cook until it starts to brown and crisp up, about 5-7 minutes.
Add the chopped kimchi, minced garlic, and ginger to the skillet. Stir-fry for another 2-3 minutes until fragrant.
Stir in the sliced onion and continue to cook for an additional 2-3 minutes until the onion softens.
In a small bowl, mix together the gochujang, soy sauce, sesame oil, and rice vinegar to make the sauce.
Pour the sauce over the pork belly and kimchi mixture in the skillet. Stir well to coat everything evenly.
Cook for another 2-3 minutes, allowing the flavors to meld together and the sauce to thicken slightly.
Once everything is heated through and well combined, remove the skillet from the heat.
Transfer the stir-fry to a serving dish and garnish with chopped green onions and sesame seeds.
Serve hot with steamed rice or on its own as a low-carb meal option. Enjoy your delicious kimchi and pork belly stir-fry!

Spicy Korean Beef Lettuce Wraps

Ingredients:

- 1 lb (450g) lean ground beef
- 1 onion, finely chopped
- 3 cloves garlic, minced
- 2 tablespoons soy sauce
- 1 tablespoon sesame oil
- 1 tablespoon gochujang (Korean chili paste)
- 1 teaspoon rice vinegar
- 1 teaspoon ginger, minced
- 1 teaspoon sugar substitute (optional, for sweetness)
- 1/2 teaspoon black pepper
- 1/4 cup water
- 1 head iceberg or butter lettuce, leaves separated
- 2 green onions, thinly sliced (for garnish)
- Toasted sesame seeds (for garnish)
- Kimchi (optional, for serving)
- Steamed rice (optional, for serving)

Instructions:

Heat a large skillet over medium heat. Add the ground beef and cook until browned, breaking it apart with a spatula as it cooks, about 5-7 minutes.
Add the chopped onion to the skillet and cook for another 2-3 minutes until the onion is translucent.
Stir in the minced garlic and cook for an additional 1-2 minutes until fragrant.
In a small bowl, whisk together the soy sauce, sesame oil, gochujang, rice vinegar, minced ginger, sugar substitute (if using), black pepper, and water to make the sauce.
Pour the sauce over the beef mixture in the skillet. Stir well to combine and let it simmer for 2-3 minutes, allowing the flavors to meld together and the sauce to slightly thicken.
Once the beef mixture is cooked through and the sauce has thickened, remove the skillet from the heat.
Spoon the spicy Korean beef onto the lettuce leaves, using them as wraps.
Garnish the wraps with thinly sliced green onions and toasted sesame seeds.
Serve with kimchi and steamed rice on the side, if desired.
Enjoy your flavorful and spicy Korean beef lettuce wraps!

Cauliflower Kimchi Fried Rice

Ingredients:

- 1 medium head of cauliflower
- 1 cup kimchi, chopped
- 2 tablespoons sesame oil
- 2 cloves garlic, minced
- 1 small onion, diced
- 1 carrot, diced
- 2 green onions, chopped
- 2 tablespoons soy sauce
- 1 tablespoon gochujang (Korean chili paste), optional
- 1 tablespoon rice vinegar
- 1 tablespoon toasted sesame seeds (for garnish)
- Salt and pepper to taste
- Cooking oil

Instructions:

Cut the cauliflower into florets, discarding the tough stems. Place the florets in a food processor and pulse until they resemble rice grains. Alternatively, you can grate the cauliflower using a box grater.
Heat a large skillet or wok over medium heat. Add a drizzle of cooking oil.
Add the minced garlic to the skillet and cook for about 1 minute until fragrant.
Add the diced onion and carrot to the skillet. Cook for 3-4 minutes until they start to soften.
Stir in the chopped kimchi and cook for another 2-3 minutes, allowing the flavors to meld together.
Push the vegetables to one side of the skillet and add a bit more oil if needed.
Add the riced cauliflower to the empty side of the skillet.
Cook the cauliflower for 4-5 minutes, stirring occasionally, until it's tender but not mushy.
In a small bowl, mix together the soy sauce, sesame oil, gochujang (if using), and rice vinegar to make the sauce.
Pour the sauce over the cauliflower and vegetables in the skillet. Stir well to combine and cook for an additional 2-3 minutes.
Season the cauliflower kimchi fried rice with salt and pepper to taste.
Remove the skillet from the heat and garnish with chopped green onions and toasted sesame seeds.

Serve hot as a flavorful and low-carb alternative to traditional fried rice. Enjoy your cauliflower kimchi fried rice!

Korean BBQ Chicken Skewers

Ingredients:

- 1 lb (450g) boneless, skinless chicken thighs, cut into 1-inch cubes
- 1/4 cup soy sauce
- 2 tablespoons honey or sugar substitute
- 2 tablespoons sesame oil
- 2 tablespoons gochujang (Korean chili paste)
- 2 cloves garlic, minced
- 1 teaspoon ginger, minced
- 1 tablespoon rice vinegar
- 1 tablespoon sesame seeds
- 2 green onions, thinly sliced (for garnish)
- Bamboo skewers, soaked in water for 30 minutes

Instructions:

In a mixing bowl, combine soy sauce, honey (or sugar substitute), sesame oil, gochujang, minced garlic, minced ginger, rice vinegar, and sesame seeds to make the marinade.

Add the chicken cubes to the marinade and toss until well coated. Cover the bowl and refrigerate for at least 1 hour, or ideally overnight, to allow the flavors to infuse.

Preheat your grill to medium-high heat or preheat your oven broiler.

Thread the marinated chicken cubes onto the soaked bamboo skewers.

If grilling, lightly oil the grill grates. Place the skewers on the grill and cook for about 5-7 minutes on each side, or until the chicken is cooked through and slightly charred.

If using the broiler, place the skewers on a foil-lined baking sheet and broil for about 6-8 minutes on each side, or until the chicken is cooked through and lightly charred.

Once cooked, remove the skewers from the heat and transfer them to a serving platter.

Garnish the Korean BBQ chicken skewers with thinly sliced green onions.

Serve hot as an appetizer or main dish, alongside steamed rice and your favorite Korean side dishes.

Enjoy your delicious Korean BBQ chicken skewers!

Zucchini Noodles with Spicy Pork Sauce

Ingredients:

- 2 medium zucchinis
- 1 lb (450g) ground pork
- 2 tablespoons sesame oil
- 3 cloves garlic, minced
- 1 small onion, finely chopped
- 1 red bell pepper, diced
- 2 tablespoons gochujang (Korean chili paste)
- 2 tablespoons soy sauce
- 1 tablespoon rice vinegar
- 1 teaspoon ginger, minced
- 1 teaspoon sugar substitute
- 1/2 cup chicken or vegetable broth
- 2 green onions, thinly sliced (for garnish)
- Sesame seeds (for garnish)
- Salt and pepper to taste
- Cooking oil

Instructions:

Using a spiralizer or a julienne peeler, create zucchini noodles (zoodles) from the zucchinis. Set aside.

Heat sesame oil in a large skillet over medium heat. Add minced garlic and cook for about 1 minute until fragrant.

Add chopped onion and diced red bell pepper to the skillet. Cook for 3-4 minutes until softened.

Add ground pork to the skillet. Break it apart with a spatula and cook until browned and cooked through, about 5-7 minutes.

In a small bowl, mix together gochujang, soy sauce, rice vinegar, minced ginger, and sugar substitute.

Pour the sauce mixture into the skillet with the cooked pork and vegetables. Stir well to combine.

Add chicken or vegetable broth to the skillet and let the sauce simmer for 5-7 minutes, allowing the flavors to meld together and the sauce to slightly thicken. Season with salt and pepper to taste.

Add the zucchini noodles to the skillet and toss until they are coated in the spicy pork sauce. Cook for an additional 2-3 minutes until the zucchini noodles are just tender.

Remove the skillet from the heat and garnish the zucchini noodles with thinly sliced green onions and sesame seeds.

Serve hot as a low-carb and flavorful alternative to traditional pasta dishes.

Enjoy your zucchini noodles with spicy pork sauce!

Korean Egg Roll Wraps

Ingredients:

- 6 large eggs
- 1/4 cup milk or water
- 1/2 cup chopped kimchi
- 1/4 cup chopped spinach
- 1/4 cup finely diced onion
- 1/4 cup shredded carrots
- 2 tablespoons chopped green onions
- 1 tablespoon soy sauce
- 1 tablespoon sesame oil
- Salt and pepper to taste
- Cooking oil

Instructions:

In a mixing bowl, whisk together the eggs and milk (or water) until well combined. Season with salt and pepper to taste.
Heat a small amount of cooking oil in a non-stick skillet over medium heat.
Pour a thin layer of the egg mixture into the skillet, tilting the pan to spread the egg evenly. Cook for 1-2 minutes until the bottom is set and lightly golden.
Sprinkle some chopped kimchi, spinach, onion, carrots, and green onions evenly over the egg in the skillet.
Drizzle a little soy sauce and sesame oil over the toppings.
Carefully roll up the egg wrap from one side to create a tight cylinder. Push it to the edge of the skillet.
Add a little more oil to the skillet if needed, then pour in another thin layer of the egg mixture to cover the empty space in the skillet.
Once the second layer of egg is cooked and set, carefully place the rolled egg wrap on top of it.
Repeat the process with the remaining egg mixture and filling ingredients until you've used up all the ingredients.
Once all the egg wraps are cooked and rolled, transfer them to a cutting board.
Use a sharp knife to slice the egg wraps into bite-sized pieces.
Serve the Korean egg roll wraps warm as an appetizer or a snack.
Enjoy your delicious and savory Korean egg roll wraps!

Tofu Kimchi Soup

Ingredients:

- 1 tablespoon sesame oil
- 1 small onion, thinly sliced
- 2 cloves garlic, minced
- 1 teaspoon ginger, minced
- 1 cup kimchi, chopped
- 4 cups vegetable or chicken broth
- 1 block (14 oz) firm tofu, cubed
- 2 tablespoons gochujang (Korean chili paste)
- 2 tablespoons soy sauce
- 2 teaspoons rice vinegar
- 2 green onions, chopped
- Salt and pepper to taste
- Optional: cooked rice, for serving

Instructions:

Heat sesame oil in a large pot over medium heat.
Add thinly sliced onion, minced garlic, and minced ginger to the pot. Sauté for 2-3 minutes until the onions are translucent and fragrant.
Add chopped kimchi to the pot and cook for another 2-3 minutes, stirring occasionally.
Pour in vegetable or chicken broth and bring the mixture to a simmer.
Add cubed tofu, gochujang, soy sauce, and rice vinegar to the pot. Stir well to combine.
Let the soup simmer for 10-15 minutes to allow the flavors to meld together.
Taste the soup and adjust seasoning with salt and pepper as needed.
Stir in chopped green onions just before serving.
Ladle the tofu kimchi soup into bowls and serve hot.
Optionally, serve the soup with cooked rice on the side.
Enjoy your comforting and flavorful tofu kimchi soup!

Beef Bulgogi Lettuce Wraps

Ingredients:

- 1 lb (450g) beef sirloin or ribeye, thinly sliced
- 1/4 cup soy sauce
- 2 tablespoons brown sugar or honey
- 2 tablespoons sesame oil
- 2 cloves garlic, minced
- 1 teaspoon ginger, minced
- 1 tablespoon rice vinegar
- 2 green onions, thinly sliced
- 1 tablespoon sesame seeds
- 1 tablespoon cooking oil
- Butter lettuce leaves, washed and separated
- Optional toppings: thinly sliced cucumber, shredded carrots, sliced avocado, kimchi

Instructions:

In a bowl, whisk together soy sauce, brown sugar (or honey), sesame oil, minced garlic, minced ginger, rice vinegar, sliced green onions, and sesame seeds to make the marinade.

Add the thinly sliced beef to the marinade, ensuring each slice is well coated.

Cover the bowl and refrigerate for at least 30 minutes, or ideally overnight, to allow the flavors to meld.

Heat cooking oil in a skillet or grill pan over medium-high heat.

Add the marinated beef slices to the skillet in a single layer, working in batches if necessary to avoid overcrowding the pan.

Cook the beef slices for 2-3 minutes on each side, or until they are caramelized and cooked to your desired level of doneness.

Once cooked, remove the beef from the skillet and transfer it to a serving platter.

To assemble the lettuce wraps, place a spoonful of beef bulgogi onto each butter lettuce leaf.

Add optional toppings such as thinly sliced cucumber, shredded carrots, sliced avocado, or kimchi on top of the beef.

Serve the beef bulgogi lettuce wraps immediately as a delicious and low-carb meal or appetizer.

Enjoy your flavorful and satisfying beef bulgogi lettuce wraps!

Korean-style Beef and Broccoli Stir-Fry

Ingredients:

- 1 lb (450g) beef sirloin or flank steak, thinly sliced
- 2 tablespoons soy sauce
- 1 tablespoon sesame oil
- 1 tablespoon brown sugar or honey
- 2 cloves garlic, minced
- 1 teaspoon ginger, minced
- 2 tablespoons cooking oil
- 1 head broccoli, cut into florets
- 1 onion, thinly sliced
- 1 red bell pepper, thinly sliced
- 2 tablespoons gochujang (Korean chili paste)
- 2 tablespoons water
- Sesame seeds (for garnish)
- Cooked rice, for serving

Instructions:

In a bowl, mix together soy sauce, sesame oil, brown sugar (or honey), minced garlic, and minced ginger to make the marinade.

Add the thinly sliced beef to the marinade and toss until well coated. Let it marinate for at least 30 minutes, or preferably overnight, in the refrigerator.

Heat 1 tablespoon of cooking oil in a large skillet or wok over medium-high heat. Add the marinated beef slices to the skillet in a single layer. Cook for 2-3 minutes on each side until browned and cooked through. Remove the beef from the skillet and set aside.

In the same skillet, add the remaining tablespoon of cooking oil. Add the sliced onion and red bell pepper to the skillet. Stir-fry for 2-3 minutes until they start to soften.

Add the broccoli florets to the skillet. Stir-fry for another 3-4 minutes until the broccoli is tender-crisp.

In a small bowl, mix together gochujang and water to make the sauce.

Return the cooked beef to the skillet. Pour the sauce over the beef and vegetables.

Stir well to combine and coat everything in the sauce. Cook for an additional 1-2 minutes until heated through.

Remove the skillet from the heat and transfer the Korean-style beef and broccoli stir-fry to a serving dish.
Garnish with sesame seeds.
Serve hot with cooked rice.
Enjoy your delicious Korean-style beef and broccoli stir-fry!

Spicy Korean Cucumber Salad

Ingredients:

- 2 medium cucumbers, thinly sliced
- 2 tablespoons gochugaru (Korean red pepper flakes)
- 1 tablespoon sesame oil
- 1 tablespoon rice vinegar
- 1 tablespoon soy sauce
- 1 tablespoon honey or sugar substitute
- 2 cloves garlic, minced
- 1 teaspoon ginger, minced
- 1 tablespoon toasted sesame seeds (for garnish)
- 2 green onions, thinly sliced (for garnish)

Instructions:

Place the thinly sliced cucumbers in a large mixing bowl.
In a separate bowl, whisk together gochugaru, sesame oil, rice vinegar, soy sauce, honey (or sugar substitute), minced garlic, and minced ginger to make the dressing.
Pour the dressing over the sliced cucumbers in the mixing bowl.
Toss the cucumbers gently until they are evenly coated in the dressing.
Cover the bowl and refrigerate for at least 30 minutes to allow the flavors to meld together.
Just before serving, garnish the spicy Korean cucumber salad with toasted sesame seeds and thinly sliced green onions.
Serve chilled as a refreshing and spicy side dish.
Enjoy your delicious spicy Korean cucumber salad!

Sesame Ginger Bok Choy Stir-Fry

Ingredients:

- 4-5 baby bok choy heads, washed and halved lengthwise
- 2 tablespoons sesame oil
- 2 cloves garlic, minced
- 1 teaspoon ginger, minced
- 2 tablespoons soy sauce
- 1 tablespoon rice vinegar
- 1 tablespoon honey or sugar substitute
- 1 tablespoon toasted sesame seeds
- Salt and pepper to taste

Instructions:

Heat sesame oil in a large skillet or wok over medium heat.

Add minced garlic and minced ginger to the skillet. Sauté for about 1 minute until fragrant.

Place the halved baby bok choy heads in the skillet, cut side down.

Cook the bok choy for 2-3 minutes until the bottoms are lightly browned and slightly softened.

In a small bowl, whisk together soy sauce, rice vinegar, and honey (or sugar substitute) to make the sauce.

Pour the sauce over the bok choy in the skillet.

Use tongs to flip the bok choy halves and coat them evenly in the sauce.

Cook for an additional 2-3 minutes until the bok choy is tender-crisp and the sauce has thickened slightly.

Season with salt and pepper to taste.

Sprinkle toasted sesame seeds over the bok choy just before serving.

Transfer the sesame ginger bok choy stir-fry to a serving dish.

Serve hot as a delicious and nutritious side dish.

Enjoy your flavorful sesame ginger bok choy stir-fry!

Korean Beef and Mushroom Skewers

Ingredients:

- 1 lb (450g) beef sirloin, cut into 1-inch cubes
- 8 oz (225g) button mushrooms
- 1/4 cup soy sauce
- 2 tablespoons sesame oil
- 2 tablespoons brown sugar or honey
- 2 cloves garlic, minced
- 1 teaspoon ginger, minced
- 1 tablespoon rice vinegar
- 1 tablespoon toasted sesame seeds
- 2 green onions, thinly sliced (for garnish)
- Bamboo skewers, soaked in water for 30 minutes

Instructions:

In a bowl, mix together soy sauce, sesame oil, brown sugar (or honey), minced garlic, minced ginger, rice vinegar, and toasted sesame seeds to make the marinade.

Add the cubed beef to the marinade and toss until well coated. Cover the bowl and refrigerate for at least 30 minutes, or preferably overnight, to allow the flavors to meld.

Clean the mushrooms and trim the stems. If they are large, cut them in half.

Preheat your grill to medium-high heat or preheat your broiler.

Thread the marinated beef cubes and mushrooms onto the soaked bamboo skewers, alternating between beef and mushrooms.

If grilling, lightly oil the grill grates. Place the skewers on the grill and cook for about 3-4 minutes on each side, or until the beef is cooked to your desired level of doneness and the mushrooms are tender.

If using the broiler, place the skewers on a foil-lined baking sheet and broil for about 4-5 minutes on each side, or until the beef is cooked through and nicely browned.

Once cooked, remove the skewers from the heat and transfer them to a serving platter.

Garnish with thinly sliced green onions.

Serve hot as a delicious and flavorful Korean-inspired appetizer or main dish.

Enjoy your tasty Korean beef and mushroom skewers!

Spicy Kimchi Cauliflower "Rice"

Ingredients:

- 1 medium head cauliflower
- 1 cup kimchi, chopped
- 2 tablespoons gochujang (Korean chili paste)
- 2 tablespoons soy sauce
- 1 tablespoon sesame oil
- 2 cloves garlic, minced
- 1 teaspoon ginger, minced
- 2 green onions, thinly sliced
- 1 tablespoon cooking oil
- Sesame seeds (for garnish)
- Optional: sliced green onions, for garnish

Instructions:

Cut the cauliflower into florets, discarding the tough stems. Place the florets in a food processor and pulse until they resemble rice grains. Alternatively, you can grate the cauliflower using a box grater.

Heat cooking oil in a large skillet or wok over medium heat.

Add minced garlic and minced ginger to the skillet. Sauté for about 1 minute until fragrant.

Add chopped kimchi to the skillet and cook for another 2-3 minutes, stirring occasionally.

Add the riced cauliflower to the skillet. Stir-fry for 4-5 minutes until the cauliflower is tender but not mushy.

In a small bowl, mix together gochujang, soy sauce, and sesame oil to make the sauce.

Pour the sauce over the cauliflower mixture in the skillet. Stir well to combine.

Cook for an additional 2-3 minutes, allowing the flavors to meld together.

Once everything is heated through and well combined, remove the skillet from the heat.

Garnish with thinly sliced green onions and sesame seeds.

Serve hot as a flavorful and spicy side dish or as a main course for a low-carb meal.

Enjoy your spicy kimchi cauliflower "rice"!

Korean BBQ Tofu Lettuce Wraps

Ingredients:

- 1 block (14 oz) firm tofu
- 2 tablespoons soy sauce
- 1 tablespoon sesame oil
- 2 tablespoons brown sugar or honey
- 2 cloves garlic, minced
- 1 teaspoon ginger, minced
- 2 tablespoons gochujang (Korean chili paste)
- 1 tablespoon rice vinegar
- 1 tablespoon cooking oil
- 1/2 cup shredded carrots
- 1/2 cup thinly sliced cucumber
- 1/4 cup chopped green onions
- Butter lettuce leaves, washed and separated
- Sesame seeds (for garnish)

Instructions:

Press the tofu to remove excess water: Place the tofu block between two paper towels and set a heavy object on top (like a plate or a skillet). Let it press for about 20-30 minutes.

In a bowl, whisk together soy sauce, sesame oil, brown sugar (or honey), minced garlic, minced ginger, gochujang, and rice vinegar to make the marinade.

Cut the pressed tofu into small cubes or rectangles.

Heat cooking oil in a large skillet over medium-high heat.

Add the tofu cubes to the skillet and cook for 5-7 minutes, stirring occasionally, until golden brown and slightly crispy on all sides.

Pour the marinade over the tofu cubes in the skillet. Stir well to coat the tofu evenly in the sauce.

Cook for another 2-3 minutes, allowing the sauce to thicken slightly and coat the tofu.

Remove the skillet from the heat and let the tofu cool slightly.

To assemble the lettuce wraps, place a spoonful of the Korean BBQ tofu onto each butter lettuce leaf.

Top the tofu with shredded carrots, thinly sliced cucumber, and chopped green onions.

Sprinkle sesame seeds over the lettuce wraps for garnish.

Serve immediately as a delicious and healthy appetizer or light meal. Enjoy your flavorful Korean BBQ tofu lettuce wraps!

Kimchi Cauliflower "Fried Rice"

Ingredients:

- 1 medium head cauliflower
- 1 cup kimchi, chopped
- 2 tablespoons soy sauce
- 1 tablespoon sesame oil
- 1 tablespoon rice vinegar
- 2 cloves garlic, minced
- 1 teaspoon ginger, minced
- 2 green onions, thinly sliced
- 1 tablespoon cooking oil
- Optional: sesame seeds for garnish

Instructions:

Cut the cauliflower into florets, discarding the tough stems. Place the florets in a food processor and pulse until they resemble rice grains. Alternatively, you can grate the cauliflower using a box grater.
Heat cooking oil in a large skillet or wok over medium heat.
Add minced garlic and minced ginger to the skillet. Sauté for about 1 minute until fragrant.
Add chopped kimchi to the skillet and cook for another 2-3 minutes, stirring occasionally.
Add the riced cauliflower to the skillet. Stir-fry for 4-5 minutes until the cauliflower is tender but not mushy.
In a small bowl, mix together soy sauce, sesame oil, and rice vinegar to make the sauce.
Pour the sauce over the cauliflower mixture in the skillet. Stir well to combine.
Cook for an additional 2-3 minutes, allowing the flavors to meld together.
Once everything is heated through and well combined, remove the skillet from the heat.
Garnish with thinly sliced green onions and sesame seeds, if desired.
Serve hot as a flavorful and low-carb alternative to traditional fried rice.
Enjoy your delicious kimchi cauliflower "fried rice"!

Stir-Fried Beef and Vegetables

Ingredients:

- 1 lb (450g) beef sirloin, thinly sliced
- 2 tablespoons soy sauce
- 1 tablespoon oyster sauce
- 1 tablespoon sesame oil
- 2 cloves garlic, minced
- 1 teaspoon ginger, minced
- 2 tablespoons cooking oil
- 1 onion, thinly sliced
- 1 bell pepper (any color), thinly sliced
- 1 cup broccoli florets
- 1 cup snow peas, trimmed
- Salt and pepper to taste
- Optional garnish: chopped green onions, sesame seeds

Instructions:

In a bowl, combine soy sauce, oyster sauce, sesame oil, minced garlic, and minced ginger to make the marinade.

Add the thinly sliced beef to the marinade. Toss until well coated and let it marinate for about 15-20 minutes.

Heat cooking oil in a large skillet or wok over high heat.

Add the marinated beef to the skillet. Stir-fry for 2-3 minutes until the beef is browned and cooked through. Remove the beef from the skillet and set aside.

In the same skillet, add a bit more oil if needed. Add thinly sliced onion, bell pepper, broccoli florets, and snow peas.

Stir-fry the vegetables for 3-4 minutes until they are tender-crisp.

Return the cooked beef to the skillet with the vegetables.

Season with salt and pepper to taste. Stir-fry everything together for another 1-2 minutes to heat through.

Once everything is heated through and well combined, remove the skillet from the heat.

Garnish with chopped green onions and sesame seeds, if desired.

Serve hot as a delicious and nutritious stir-fried beef and vegetable dish.

Enjoy your flavorful stir-fried beef and vegetables!

Korean-style Spicy Grilled Shrimp
Ingredients:

- 1 lb (450g) large shrimp, peeled and deveined
- 2 tablespoons soy sauce
- 1 tablespoon sesame oil
- 1 tablespoon gochujang (Korean chili paste)
- 2 cloves garlic, minced
- 1 teaspoon ginger, minced
- 1 tablespoon honey or sugar substitute
- 1 tablespoon rice vinegar
- 1 tablespoon cooking oil
- Optional garnish: sliced green onions, toasted sesame seeds

Instructions:

In a bowl, mix together soy sauce, sesame oil, gochujang, minced garlic, minced ginger, honey (or sugar substitute), and rice vinegar to make the marinade.
Add the peeled and deveined shrimp to the marinade. Toss until well coated and let them marinate for about 15-20 minutes.
Preheat your grill to medium-high heat.
Thread the marinated shrimp onto skewers, if using.
Brush the grill grates with cooking oil to prevent sticking.
Place the shrimp skewers on the preheated grill. Cook for 2-3 minutes on each side until the shrimp are pink and opaque.
While grilling, you can brush the shrimp with any remaining marinade for extra flavor.
Once the shrimp are cooked through, remove them from the grill and transfer them to a serving platter.
Garnish with sliced green onions and toasted sesame seeds, if desired.
Serve hot as a delicious and spicy Korean-style grilled shrimp appetizer or main dish.
Enjoy your flavorful and spicy grilled shrimp!

Eggplant Kimchi Stir-Fry

Ingredients:

- 1 large eggplant, cut into cubes or slices
- 1 cup kimchi, chopped
- 2 tablespoons gochujang (Korean chili paste)
- 1 tablespoon soy sauce
- 1 tablespoon sesame oil
- 2 cloves garlic, minced
- 1 teaspoon ginger, minced
- 1 tablespoon rice vinegar
- 1 tablespoon cooking oil
- 2 green onions, thinly sliced (for garnish)
- Sesame seeds (for garnish)

Instructions:

Heat cooking oil in a large skillet or wok over medium-high heat.

Add minced garlic and minced ginger to the skillet. Sauté for about 1 minute until fragrant.

Add chopped kimchi to the skillet and cook for another 2-3 minutes, stirring occasionally.

Add the cubed or sliced eggplant to the skillet. Stir-fry for 4-5 minutes until the eggplant is tender but not mushy.

In a small bowl, mix together gochujang, soy sauce, sesame oil, and rice vinegar to make the sauce.

Pour the sauce over the eggplant mixture in the skillet. Stir well to combine.

Cook for an additional 2-3 minutes, allowing the flavors to meld together.

Once everything is heated through and well combined, remove the skillet from the heat.

Garnish with thinly sliced green onions and sesame seeds.

Serve hot as a flavorful and spicy eggplant kimchi stir-fry.

Enjoy your delicious Korean-inspired eggplant kimchi stir-fry!

Korean-style Beef Zucchini Noodles

Ingredients:

- 1 lb (450g) beef sirloin or flank steak, thinly sliced
- 3 medium zucchinis
- 2 tablespoons soy sauce
- 1 tablespoon sesame oil
- 1 tablespoon gochujang (Korean chili paste)
- 1 tablespoon honey or sugar substitute
- 2 cloves garlic, minced
- 1 teaspoon ginger, minced
- 1 tablespoon rice vinegar
- 2 green onions, thinly sliced
- Sesame seeds (for garnish)
- Cooking oil

Instructions:

Cut the zucchinis into noodles using a spiralizer or julienne peeler. Set aside.
In a bowl, mix together soy sauce, sesame oil, gochujang, honey (or sugar substitute), minced garlic, minced ginger, and rice vinegar to make the marinade.
Add the thinly sliced beef to the marinade. Toss until well coated and let it marinate for about 15-20 minutes.
Heat a bit of cooking oil in a large skillet or wok over medium-high heat.
Add the marinated beef to the skillet. Stir-fry for 3-4 minutes until the beef is browned and cooked through. Remove the beef from the skillet and set aside.
In the same skillet, add a bit more oil if needed. Add the zucchini noodles to the skillet.
Stir-fry the zucchini noodles for 2-3 minutes until they are just tender but still crisp.
Return the cooked beef to the skillet with the zucchini noodles.
Stir in thinly sliced green onions and toss everything together for another minute to heat through.
Once everything is heated through and well combined, remove the skillet from the heat.
Garnish with sesame seeds.
Serve hot as a delicious and low-carb Korean-style beef zucchini noodle dish.
Enjoy your flavorful and nutritious Korean-style beef zucchini noodles!

Spicy Korean Chicken Drumsticks

Ingredients:

- 8 chicken drumsticks
- 1/4 cup soy sauce
- 2 tablespoons gochujang (Korean chili paste)
- 2 tablespoons honey or sugar substitute
- 1 tablespoon sesame oil
- 2 cloves garlic, minced
- 1 teaspoon ginger, minced
- 1 tablespoon rice vinegar
- 1 tablespoon cooking oil
- Sesame seeds (for garnish)
- Sliced green onions (for garnish)

Instructions:

In a bowl, whisk together soy sauce, gochujang, honey (or sugar substitute), sesame oil, minced garlic, minced ginger, and rice vinegar to make the marinade.
Place the chicken drumsticks in a large resealable plastic bag or a shallow dish. Pour the marinade over the chicken drumsticks, making sure they are well coated. Seal the bag or cover the dish and refrigerate for at least 1 hour, or ideally overnight, to marinate.
Preheat your oven to 400°F (200°C). Line a baking sheet with aluminum foil and grease it lightly with cooking oil.
Remove the chicken drumsticks from the marinade, shaking off any excess, and place them on the prepared baking sheet.
Bake the chicken drumsticks in the preheated oven for 30-35 minutes, turning halfway through, or until they are cooked through and the skin is crispy and golden brown.
While the chicken is baking, transfer the remaining marinade to a small saucepan. Bring it to a simmer over medium heat and cook for 5-7 minutes until it thickens into a sauce.
Once the chicken drumsticks are cooked, remove them from the oven and brush them with the thickened sauce.
Garnish the spicy Korean chicken drumsticks with sesame seeds and sliced green onions.
Serve hot as a delicious and flavorful main dish.

Enjoy your spicy Korean chicken drumsticks!

Sesame Cauliflower Rice with Beef

Ingredients:

- 1 lb (450g) ground beef
- 1 medium head cauliflower
- 2 tablespoons soy sauce
- 1 tablespoon sesame oil
- 1 tablespoon rice vinegar
- 1 tablespoon honey or sugar substitute
- 2 cloves garlic, minced
- 1 teaspoon ginger, minced
- 2 green onions, thinly sliced
- Sesame seeds (for garnish)
- Cooking oil
- Salt and pepper to taste

Instructions:

Cut the cauliflower into florets, discarding the tough stems. Place the florets in a food processor and pulse until they resemble rice grains. Alternatively, you can grate the cauliflower using a box grater.

In a small bowl, mix together soy sauce, sesame oil, rice vinegar, honey (or sugar substitute), minced garlic, and minced ginger to make the sauce.

Heat a bit of cooking oil in a large skillet or wok over medium-high heat.

Add the ground beef to the skillet. Cook, breaking it apart with a spatula, until it is browned and cooked through.

Push the cooked beef to one side of the skillet and add the riced cauliflower to the other side.

Cook the cauliflower for 4-5 minutes, stirring occasionally, until it is tender but not mushy.

Pour the sauce over the cauliflower and beef mixture in the skillet. Stir well to combine.

Cook for another 2-3 minutes, allowing the flavors to meld together.

Season with salt and pepper to taste.

Once everything is heated through and well combined, remove the skillet from the heat.

Garnish with thinly sliced green onions and sesame seeds.

Serve hot as a flavorful and nutritious sesame cauliflower rice with beef dish.

Enjoy your delicious sesame cauliflower rice with beef!

Korean Beef and Vegetable Stir-Fry

Ingredients:

- 1 lb (450g) beef sirloin or flank steak, thinly sliced
- 2 tablespoons soy sauce
- 1 tablespoon sesame oil
- 1 tablespoon brown sugar or honey
- 2 cloves garlic, minced
- 1 teaspoon ginger, minced
- 2 tablespoons cooking oil
- 1 onion, thinly sliced
- 1 bell pepper (any color), thinly sliced
- 1 cup broccoli florets
- 1 cup snow peas, trimmed
- 1 carrot, julienned
- Salt and pepper to taste
- Cooked rice, for serving
- Optional garnish: sliced green onions, sesame seeds

Instructions:

In a bowl, mix together soy sauce, sesame oil, brown sugar (or honey), minced garlic, and minced ginger to make the marinade.

Add the thinly sliced beef to the marinade. Toss until well coated and let it marinate for about 15-20 minutes.

Heat a bit of cooking oil in a large skillet or wok over high heat.

Add the marinated beef to the skillet. Stir-fry for 2-3 minutes until the beef is browned and cooked through. Remove the beef from the skillet and set aside.

In the same skillet, add a bit more oil if needed. Add thinly sliced onion, bell pepper, broccoli florets, snow peas, and julienned carrot.

Stir-fry the vegetables for 3-4 minutes until they are tender-crisp.

Return the cooked beef to the skillet with the vegetables.

Season with salt and pepper to taste. Stir-fry everything together for another 1-2 minutes to heat through.

Once everything is heated through and well combined, remove the skillet from the heat.

Serve the Korean beef and vegetable stir-fry over cooked rice.

Garnish with sliced green onions and sesame seeds, if desired.

Enjoy your flavorful Korean beef and vegetable stir-fry!

Spicy Kimchi Tofu Stir-Fry
Ingredients:

- 1 block (14 oz) firm tofu, pressed and cubed
- 1 cup kimchi, chopped
- 2 tablespoons gochujang (Korean chili paste)
- 2 tablespoons soy sauce
- 1 tablespoon sesame oil
- 2 cloves garlic, minced
- 1 teaspoon ginger, minced
- 2 green onions, thinly sliced
- 1 tablespoon cooking oil
- Optional: sesame seeds for garnish

Instructions:

Heat cooking oil in a large skillet or wok over medium-high heat.
Add minced garlic and minced ginger to the skillet. Sauté for about 1 minute until fragrant.
Add chopped kimchi to the skillet and cook for another 2-3 minutes, stirring occasionally.
Add the cubed tofu to the skillet. Stir-fry for 4-5 minutes until the tofu is lightly browned on all sides.
In a small bowl, mix together gochujang, soy sauce, and sesame oil to make the sauce.
Pour the sauce over the tofu and kimchi in the skillet. Stir well to combine.
Cook for an additional 2-3 minutes, allowing the flavors to meld together.
Once everything is heated through and well combined, remove the skillet from the heat.
Garnish with thinly sliced green onions and sesame seeds, if desired.
Serve hot as a flavorful and spicy kimchi tofu stir-fry.
Enjoy your delicious and spicy kimchi tofu stir-fry!

Korean-style Cabbage and Beef Stir-Fry

Ingredients:

- 1 lb (450g) ground beef
- 1 small head cabbage, thinly sliced
- 1 onion, thinly sliced
- 2 carrots, julienned
- 2 cloves garlic, minced
- 1 tablespoon ginger, minced
- 2 tablespoons soy sauce
- 1 tablespoon sesame oil
- 1 tablespoon gochujang (Korean chili paste)
- 1 tablespoon honey or sugar substitute
- 2 green onions, thinly sliced (for garnish)
- Cooking oil
- Salt and pepper to taste

Instructions:

Heat a bit of cooking oil in a large skillet or wok over medium-high heat.
Add minced garlic and minced ginger to the skillet. Sauté for about 1 minute until fragrant.
Add ground beef to the skillet. Cook, breaking it apart with a spatula, until it is browned and cooked through.
Push the cooked beef to one side of the skillet and add sliced onion and julienned carrots to the other side. Stir-fry for 2-3 minutes until they begin to soften.
Add thinly sliced cabbage to the skillet. Stir-fry everything together for another 3-4 minutes until the cabbage is wilted and tender.
In a small bowl, mix together soy sauce, sesame oil, gochujang, and honey (or sugar substitute) to make the sauce.
Pour the sauce over the cabbage and beef mixture in the skillet. Stir well to combine.
Cook for another 2-3 minutes, allowing the flavors to meld together.
Season with salt and pepper to taste.
Once everything is heated through and well combined, remove the skillet from the heat.
Garnish with thinly sliced green onions.
Serve hot as a delicious and nutritious Korean-style cabbage and beef stir-fry.

Enjoy your flavorful and satisfying meal!

Low-Carb Kimchi Pancakes

Ingredients:

- 1 cup kimchi, chopped
- 4 large eggs
- 1/4 cup almond flour
- 2 tablespoons coconut flour
- 2 green onions, thinly sliced
- 1 tablespoon soy sauce or tamari
- 1 teaspoon sesame oil
- Cooking oil (for frying)
- Optional: sliced green onions and sesame seeds for garnish

Instructions:

In a mixing bowl, combine chopped kimchi, eggs, almond flour, coconut flour, thinly sliced green onions, soy sauce, and sesame oil. Mix until well combined.
Heat a bit of cooking oil in a non-stick skillet or frying pan over medium heat.
Once the skillet is hot, pour a portion of the kimchi pancake batter into the skillet, spreading it out into a thin, even layer.
Cook the pancake for about 3-4 minutes on each side, until golden brown and crispy.
Repeat the process with the remaining batter, adding more oil to the skillet as needed.
Once all the pancakes are cooked, transfer them to a serving plate.
Garnish with sliced green onions and sesame seeds, if desired.
Serve the low-carb kimchi pancakes hot as a delicious appetizer or snack.
Enjoy your tasty and nutritious low-carb kimchi pancakes!

Spicy Korean Radish Salad

Ingredients:

- 2 cups daikon radish, julienned
- 2 tablespoons gochugaru (Korean red pepper flakes)
- 1 tablespoon sesame oil
- 1 tablespoon rice vinegar
- 1 tablespoon soy sauce
- 1 tablespoon honey or sugar substitute
- 2 cloves garlic, minced
- 1 teaspoon ginger, minced
- 2 green onions, thinly sliced
- Sesame seeds (for garnish)

Instructions:

In a large mixing bowl, combine julienned daikon radish, minced garlic, minced ginger, and thinly sliced green onions.

In a separate bowl, whisk together gochugaru, sesame oil, rice vinegar, soy sauce, and honey (or sugar substitute) to make the dressing.

Pour the dressing over the daikon radish mixture in the mixing bowl.

Toss until the daikon radish is evenly coated in the dressing.

Cover the bowl and refrigerate for at least 30 minutes to allow the flavors to meld together.

Just before serving, garnish the spicy Korean radish salad with sesame seeds.

Serve chilled as a refreshing and spicy side dish.

Enjoy your delicious spicy Korean radish salad!

Korean Beef Lettuce Wraps with Pickled Vegetables

Ingredients:

For the Korean Beef:

- 1 lb (450g) ground beef
- 2 tablespoons soy sauce
- 1 tablespoon sesame oil
- 2 cloves garlic, minced
- 1 teaspoon ginger, minced
- 1 tablespoon brown sugar or honey
- 2 green onions, thinly sliced
- 1 tablespoon cooking oil
- Salt and pepper to taste

For the Pickled Vegetables:

- 1 carrot, julienned
- 1 cucumber, julienned
- 1/2 cup rice vinegar
- 1 tablespoon sugar
- 1 teaspoon salt

For Serving:

- Butter lettuce leaves
- Cooked rice (optional)
- Sriracha or gochujang (Korean chili paste) for extra spice (optional)
- Sesame seeds for garnish (optional)

Instructions:

Start by preparing the pickled vegetables. In a bowl, mix together rice vinegar, sugar, and salt until the sugar and salt are dissolved. Add the julienned carrot and cucumber to the bowl, ensuring they are fully submerged in the vinegar mixture. Cover and refrigerate for at least 30 minutes, or overnight for best results.

In a small bowl, mix together soy sauce, sesame oil, minced garlic, minced ginger, and brown sugar (or honey) to make the marinade for the beef.

Heat cooking oil in a large skillet over medium-high heat. Add the ground beef to the skillet and cook until browned, breaking it apart with a spatula as it cooks.

Once the beef is browned, add the marinade to the skillet. Stir well to coat the beef evenly in the sauce. Cook for an additional 2-3 minutes, allowing the flavors to meld together. Taste and adjust seasoning with salt and pepper if needed.
While the beef is cooking, prepare the lettuce leaves for serving. Wash and dry the lettuce leaves, then arrange them on a serving platter.
Once the beef is cooked and the pickled vegetables are ready, assemble the lettuce wraps. Spoon some cooked rice (if using) onto each lettuce leaf, followed by a spoonful of the Korean beef and some pickled vegetables.
Optional: Drizzle some sriracha or add a dollop of gochujang on top of the beef for extra spice.
Garnish with thinly sliced green onions and sesame seeds if desired.
Serve immediately and enjoy your delicious Korean beef lettuce wraps with pickled vegetables!

Tofu and Vegetable Bibimbap Bowls

Ingredients:

For the Tofu:

- 1 block (14 oz) firm tofu, pressed and cubed
- 2 tablespoons soy sauce
- 1 tablespoon sesame oil
- 1 tablespoon gochujang (Korean chili paste)
- 1 tablespoon honey or sugar substitute
- 2 cloves garlic, minced
- 1 teaspoon ginger, minced
- 1 tablespoon rice vinegar
- Cooking oil (for frying)

For the Vegetables:

- 2 cups cooked short-grain rice
- 2 cups spinach
- 1 carrot, julienned
- 1 zucchini, julienned
- 1 cup bean sprouts
- 1 tablespoon sesame oil
- Salt, to taste

For the Bibimbap Sauce:

- 2 tablespoons gochujang (Korean chili paste)
- 1 tablespoon soy sauce
- 1 tablespoon rice vinegar
- 1 teaspoon sesame oil
- 1 teaspoon honey or sugar substitute
- 1 clove garlic, minced

Optional Toppings:

- Fried eggs
- Kimchi
- Sesame seeds
- Sliced green onions

Instructions:

Start by preparing the tofu. In a bowl, mix together soy sauce, sesame oil, gochujang, honey (or sugar substitute), minced garlic, minced ginger, and rice vinegar to make the marinade. Add the cubed tofu to the marinade and let it marinate for at least 15-20 minutes.

While the tofu is marinating, cook the rice according to package instructions.

In a separate bowl, mix together all the ingredients for the bibimbap sauce. Set aside.

Heat a bit of cooking oil in a large skillet over medium-high heat. Add the marinated tofu cubes to the skillet and cook until browned and crispy on all sides, about 5-7 minutes. Remove the tofu from the skillet and set aside.

In the same skillet, add a bit more oil if needed. Stir-fry the spinach until wilted, then season with a bit of salt. Remove from the skillet and set aside.

Repeat the process with the julienned carrot, zucchini, and bean sprouts, stir-frying each vegetable separately until just tender. Season each vegetable with a bit of salt as you cook. Set aside.

To assemble the bibimbap bowls, divide the cooked rice among serving bowls. Arrange the cooked tofu and stir-fried vegetables on top of the rice.

Drizzle the bibimbap sauce over the tofu and vegetables.

Optional: Top each bowl with a fried egg and serve with kimchi on the side.

Garnish with sesame seeds and sliced green onions if desired.

Serve immediately and enjoy your delicious tofu and vegetable bibimbap bowls!

Korean-style Cucumber Noodle Salad

Ingredients:

For the Salad:

- 2 English cucumbers
- 1 carrot, julienned
- 2 green onions, thinly sliced
- 2 tablespoons chopped fresh cilantro or parsley
- Sesame seeds, for garnish

For the Dressing:

- 2 tablespoons soy sauce
- 1 tablespoon rice vinegar
- 1 tablespoon sesame oil
- 1 tablespoon honey or sugar substitute
- 1 teaspoon grated ginger
- 1 clove garlic, minced
- 1/2 teaspoon gochugaru (Korean chili flakes), optional for spice

Instructions:

Using a vegetable spiralizer, spiralize the English cucumbers into noodles. Alternatively, you can use a julienne peeler to create cucumber strips.

In a large bowl, combine the cucumber noodles, julienned carrot, thinly sliced green onions, and chopped fresh cilantro or parsley.

In a small bowl, whisk together the soy sauce, rice vinegar, sesame oil, honey (or sugar substitute), grated ginger, minced garlic, and gochugaru (if using) to make the dressing.

Pour the dressing over the cucumber noodle mixture in the large bowl. Toss until everything is evenly coated in the dressing.

Let the salad sit for about 10-15 minutes to allow the flavors to meld together and the cucumber noodles to soften slightly.

Transfer the salad to a serving dish and sprinkle sesame seeds on top for garnish.

Serve the Korean-style cucumber noodle salad as a refreshing side dish or light meal.
Enjoy your delicious and healthy salad!

Spicy Korean Pork and Cabbage Stir-Fry

Ingredients:

- 1 lb (450g) pork tenderloin or pork shoulder, thinly sliced
- 4 cups cabbage, thinly sliced
- 1 onion, thinly sliced
- 2 carrots, julienned
- 3 cloves garlic, minced
- 1 teaspoon ginger, minced
- 2 tablespoons soy sauce
- 1 tablespoon gochujang (Korean chili paste)
- 1 tablespoon sesame oil
- 1 tablespoon honey or sugar substitute
- 2 green onions, thinly sliced (for garnish)
- Cooking oil
- Sesame seeds (for garnish, optional)
- Cooked rice, for serving

Instructions:

In a bowl, mix together soy sauce, gochujang, sesame oil, and honey (or sugar substitute) to make the sauce. Set aside.
Heat a bit of cooking oil in a large skillet or wok over medium-high heat.
Add minced garlic and minced ginger to the skillet. Sauté for about 1 minute until fragrant.
Add thinly sliced pork to the skillet. Stir-fry for 3-4 minutes until the pork is browned and cooked through. Remove the pork from the skillet and set aside.
In the same skillet, add a bit more oil if needed. Add thinly sliced onion and julienned carrots. Stir-fry for 2-3 minutes until they begin to soften.
Add thinly sliced cabbage to the skillet. Stir-fry everything together for another 3-4 minutes until the cabbage is wilted and tender.
Return the cooked pork to the skillet with the vegetables.
Pour the sauce over the pork and vegetables in the skillet. Stir well to combine.
Cook for another 2-3 minutes, allowing the flavors to meld together.
Once everything is heated through and well combined, remove the skillet from the heat.
Garnish with thinly sliced green onions and sesame seeds, if desired.

Serve hot over cooked rice as a delicious and spicy Korean pork and cabbage stir-fry.
Enjoy your flavorful and satisfying meal!

Korean-style Beef and Pepper Skewers

Ingredients:

- 1 lb (450g) beef sirloin or flank steak, thinly sliced
- 2 bell peppers (any color), cut into chunks
- 1 onion, cut into chunks
- For the Marinade:
    - 3 tablespoons soy sauce
    - 1 tablespoon sesame oil
    - 1 tablespoon honey or sugar substitute
    - 2 cloves garlic, minced
    - 1 teaspoon ginger, minced
    - 1 tablespoon rice vinegar
    - 1 tablespoon gochujang (Korean chili paste), optional for spice
- Skewers, soaked in water if wooden

Instructions:

In a bowl, whisk together soy sauce, sesame oil, honey (or sugar substitute), minced garlic, minced ginger, rice vinegar, and gochujang (if using) to make the marinade.

Add thinly sliced beef to the marinade. Toss until well coated and let it marinate for about 30 minutes to 1 hour in the refrigerator.

Preheat your grill or grill pan to medium-high heat.

Thread the marinated beef, bell peppers, and onions onto the skewers, alternating between beef and vegetables.

Place the skewers on the preheated grill. Cook for 3-4 minutes on each side, or until the beef is cooked to your desired doneness and the vegetables are tender.

While grilling, you can brush the skewers with any remaining marinade for extra flavor.

Once the skewers are cooked, remove them from the grill and transfer them to a serving platter.

Serve hot as a delicious and flavorful Korean-style beef and pepper skewers.

Enjoy your tasty skewers with rice or your favorite side dishes!

Cauliflower Kimchi "Fried Rice"

Ingredients:

- 1 medium head cauliflower
- 1 cup kimchi, chopped
- 2 cloves garlic, minced
- 2 green onions, thinly sliced
- 2 eggs, beaten
- 2 tablespoons soy sauce
- 1 tablespoon sesame oil
- 1 tablespoon gochujang (Korean chili paste), optional for extra spice
- 1 tablespoon cooking oil
- Sesame seeds, for garnish (optional)

Instructions:

Cut the cauliflower into florets and place them in a food processor. Pulse until the cauliflower resembles rice grains, or use a box grater to grate the cauliflower into rice-like pieces. Set aside.

Heat cooking oil in a large skillet or wok over medium-high heat.

Add minced garlic to the skillet and sauté for about 1 minute until fragrant.

Add chopped kimchi to the skillet and cook for another 2-3 minutes, stirring occasionally.

Add the cauliflower rice to the skillet and stir-fry for 4-5 minutes until it is tender but not mushy.

Push the cauliflower rice to one side of the skillet and add beaten eggs to the other side. Scramble the eggs until cooked through.

Once the eggs are cooked, mix them into the cauliflower rice in the skillet.

Stir in thinly sliced green onions, soy sauce, sesame oil, and gochujang (if using). Mix everything together until well combined.

Cook for another 2-3 minutes to heat through and allow the flavors to meld together.

Once everything is heated through and well combined, remove the skillet from the heat.

Garnish with sesame seeds, if desired.

Serve hot as a delicious and low-carb cauliflower kimchi "fried rice".

Enjoy your flavorful and nutritious dish!

Spicy Korean Beef and Cabbage Stir-Fry

Ingredients:

- 1 lb (450g) ground beef
- 4 cups cabbage, thinly sliced
- 1 onion, thinly sliced
- 2 carrots, julienned
- 3 cloves garlic, minced
- 1 teaspoon ginger, minced
- 2 tablespoons soy sauce
- 1 tablespoon gochujang (Korean chili paste)
- 1 tablespoon sesame oil
- 1 tablespoon honey or sugar substitute
- 2 green onions, thinly sliced (for garnish)
- Cooking oil
- Sesame seeds (for garnish, optional)
- Cooked rice, for serving

Instructions:

Heat a bit of cooking oil in a large skillet or wok over medium-high heat.
Add minced garlic and minced ginger to the skillet. Sauté for about 1 minute until fragrant.
Add ground beef to the skillet. Cook, breaking it apart with a spatula, until it is browned and cooked through.
Push the cooked beef to one side of the skillet and add thinly sliced onion and julienned carrots to the other side. Stir-fry for 2-3 minutes until they begin to soften.
Add thinly sliced cabbage to the skillet. Stir-fry everything together for another 3-4 minutes until the cabbage is wilted and tender.
In a small bowl, mix together soy sauce, gochujang, sesame oil, and honey (or sugar substitute) to make the sauce.
Pour the sauce over the beef and vegetables in the skillet. Stir well to combine. Cook for another 2-3 minutes, allowing the flavors to meld together.
Once everything is heated through and well combined, remove the skillet from the heat.
Garnish with thinly sliced green onions and sesame seeds, if desired.

Serve hot over cooked rice as a delicious and spicy Korean beef and cabbage stir-fry.
Enjoy your flavorful and satisfying meal!

Korean-style Sesame Green Beans

Ingredients:

- 1 lb (450g) green beans, trimmed
- 2 tablespoons soy sauce
- 1 tablespoon sesame oil
- 1 tablespoon rice vinegar
- 1 tablespoon honey or sugar substitute
- 2 cloves garlic, minced
- 1 teaspoon ginger, minced
- 1 tablespoon sesame seeds
- Cooking oil
- Salt, to taste
- Optional: sliced green onions for garnish

Instructions:

Bring a large pot of salted water to a boil. Add the green beans and blanch them for about 2-3 minutes, or until they are crisp-tender. Drain the green beans and immediately transfer them to a bowl of ice water to stop the cooking process. Drain again and pat dry with paper towels.
In a small bowl, whisk together soy sauce, sesame oil, rice vinegar, honey (or sugar substitute), minced garlic, and minced ginger to make the sauce.
Heat a bit of cooking oil in a large skillet or wok over medium-high heat.
Add the blanched green beans to the skillet. Stir-fry for 2-3 minutes until they are heated through.
Pour the sauce over the green beans in the skillet. Stir well to coat the green beans evenly in the sauce.
Cook for another 1-2 minutes, allowing the flavors to meld together.
Once the green beans are coated in the sauce and heated through, remove the skillet from the heat.
Transfer the green beans to a serving dish.
Sprinkle sesame seeds over the green beans.
Optional: Garnish with sliced green onions.
Serve hot as a delicious and flavorful Korean-style sesame green beans.
Enjoy your tasty and nutritious side dish!

Low-Carb Korean BBQ Beef Bowls

Ingredients:

For the Beef:

- 1 lb (450g) beef sirloin or flank steak, thinly sliced
- 2 tablespoons soy sauce
- 1 tablespoon sesame oil
- 1 tablespoon brown sugar or sugar substitute
- 2 cloves garlic, minced
- 1 teaspoon ginger, minced
- 1 tablespoon rice vinegar
- 2 green onions, thinly sliced (for garnish)
- Sesame seeds (for garnish, optional)
- Cooking oil

For the Cauliflower Rice:

- 1 medium head cauliflower
- 2 tablespoons soy sauce
- 1 tablespoon sesame oil
- 2 cloves garlic, minced
- 1 teaspoon ginger, minced
- 2 green onions, thinly sliced (for garnish)

Instructions:

Start by preparing the cauliflower rice. Cut the cauliflower into florets and place them in a food processor. Pulse until the cauliflower resembles rice grains, or use a box grater to grate the cauliflower into rice-like pieces.

Heat a bit of cooking oil in a large skillet or wok over medium-high heat.

Add minced garlic and minced ginger to the skillet. Sauté for about 1 minute until fragrant.

Add the cauliflower rice to the skillet. Stir-fry for 4-5 minutes until it is tender but not mushy.

Push the cauliflower rice to one side of the skillet and add thinly sliced green onions to the other side. Stir-fry for another minute.

In a small bowl, mix together soy sauce and sesame oil. Pour the mixture over the cauliflower rice. Stir well to combine. Cook for another 1-2 minutes, then remove from heat.

In a separate bowl, mix together soy sauce, sesame oil, brown sugar (or sugar substitute), minced garlic, minced ginger, and rice vinegar to make the marinade for the beef.

Add thinly sliced beef to the marinade. Toss until well coated and let it marinate for about 15-20 minutes.

Heat a bit of cooking oil in a large skillet or wok over medium-high heat.

Add the marinated beef to the skillet. Stir-fry for 3-4 minutes until the beef is browned and cooked through.

Once the beef is cooked, assemble the bowls by dividing the cauliflower rice among serving bowls. Top with the cooked beef.

Garnish with thinly sliced green onions and sesame seeds, if desired.

Serve hot as a delicious and low-carb Korean BBQ beef bowl.

Enjoy your flavorful and satisfying meal!

Spicy Kimchi Chicken Stir-Fry

Ingredients:

- 1 lb (450g) boneless, skinless chicken breast or thighs, thinly sliced
- 1 cup kimchi, chopped
- 2 tablespoons gochujang (Korean chili paste)
- 2 tablespoons soy sauce
- 1 tablespoon sesame oil
- 1 tablespoon honey or sugar substitute
- 2 cloves garlic, minced
- 1 teaspoon ginger, minced
- 1 tablespoon rice vinegar
- 2 green onions, thinly sliced (for garnish)
- Cooking oil
- Sesame seeds (for garnish, optional)

Instructions:

In a bowl, mix together gochujang, soy sauce, sesame oil, honey (or sugar substitute), minced garlic, minced ginger, and rice vinegar to make the sauce.

Heat a bit of cooking oil in a large skillet or wok over medium-high heat.

Add thinly sliced chicken to the skillet. Stir-fry for 4-5 minutes until the chicken is browned and cooked through.

Push the cooked chicken to one side of the skillet and add chopped kimchi to the other side. Cook for 2-3 minutes, stirring occasionally.

Once the kimchi is heated through, combine it with the chicken in the skillet.

Pour the sauce over the chicken and kimchi in the skillet. Stir well to combine.

Cook for another 2-3 minutes, allowing the flavors to meld together.

Once everything is heated through and well combined, remove the skillet from the heat.

Garnish with thinly sliced green onions and sesame seeds, if desired.

Serve hot as a delicious and spicy kimchi chicken stir-fry.

Enjoy your flavorful and satisfying meal!

Korean Beef and Spinach Stir-Fry

Ingredients:

- 1 lb (450g) beef sirloin or flank steak, thinly sliced
- 4 cups spinach leaves
- 1 onion, thinly sliced
- 2 cloves garlic, minced
- 1 teaspoon ginger, minced
- 2 tablespoons soy sauce
- 1 tablespoon sesame oil
- 1 tablespoon brown sugar or sugar substitute
- 1 tablespoon rice vinegar
- 2 green onions, thinly sliced (for garnish)
- Cooking oil
- Sesame seeds (for garnish, optional)

Instructions:

In a bowl, mix together soy sauce, sesame oil, brown sugar (or sugar substitute), minced garlic, minced ginger, and rice vinegar to make the marinade.

Add thinly sliced beef to the marinade. Toss until well coated and let it marinate for about 15-20 minutes.

Heat a bit of cooking oil in a large skillet or wok over medium-high heat.

Add thinly sliced onion to the skillet. Stir-fry for 2-3 minutes until the onion begins to soften.

Add the marinated beef to the skillet. Stir-fry for 4-5 minutes until the beef is browned and cooked through.

Add spinach leaves to the skillet. Stir-fry for another 1-2 minutes until the spinach is wilted.

Once everything is cooked through and well combined, remove the skillet from the heat.

Garnish with thinly sliced green onions and sesame seeds, if desired.

Serve hot as a delicious and nutritious Korean beef and spinach stir-fry.

Enjoy your flavorful and satisfying meal!

Spicy Tofu Kimchi Soup

Ingredients:

- 1 tablespoon sesame oil
- 1 onion, thinly sliced
- 2 cloves garlic, minced
- 1 teaspoon ginger, minced
- 1 cup kimchi, chopped
- 4 cups vegetable or chicken broth
- 1 block (14 oz) firm tofu, cut into cubes
- 2 tablespoons gochujang (Korean chili paste)
- 2 tablespoons soy sauce
- 1 tablespoon rice vinegar
- 2 green onions, thinly sliced (for garnish)
- Cooked rice, for serving (optional)
- Sesame seeds (for garnish, optional)

Instructions:

Heat sesame oil in a large pot over medium heat.
Add thinly sliced onion, minced garlic, and minced ginger to the pot. Sauté for 2-3 minutes until the onion is translucent and fragrant.
Add chopped kimchi to the pot. Cook for another 2-3 minutes, stirring occasionally.
Pour vegetable or chicken broth into the pot. Bring to a simmer.
Once simmering, add cubed tofu to the pot.
In a small bowl, mix together gochujang, soy sauce, and rice vinegar. Add the mixture to the pot and stir well to combine.
Let the soup simmer for 10-15 minutes, allowing the flavors to meld together and the tofu to absorb the flavors.
Taste the soup and adjust seasoning if needed.
Once the soup is ready, ladle it into bowls.
Garnish each bowl with thinly sliced green onions and sesame seeds, if desired.
Serve hot as a delicious and spicy tofu kimchi soup.
Optionally, serve with cooked rice on the side for a more filling meal.
Enjoy your flavorful and comforting soup!

Korean-style Stir-Fried Shrimp and Vegetables
Ingredients:

- 1 lb (450g) large shrimp, peeled and deveined
- 2 cups mixed vegetables (such as bell peppers, broccoli, carrots, snap peas)
- 2 cloves garlic, minced
- 1 teaspoon ginger, minced
- 2 tablespoons soy sauce
- 1 tablespoon sesame oil
- 1 tablespoon honey or sugar substitute
- 1 tablespoon rice vinegar
- 2 green onions, thinly sliced (for garnish)
- Cooking oil
- Sesame seeds (for garnish, optional)

Instructions:

Heat a bit of cooking oil in a large skillet or wok over medium-high heat.
Add minced garlic and minced ginger to the skillet. Sauté for about 1 minute until fragrant.
Add mixed vegetables to the skillet. Stir-fry for 3-4 minutes until they begin to soften.
Push the vegetables to one side of the skillet and add the peeled and deveined shrimp to the other side. Stir-fry for 2-3 minutes until the shrimp turn pink and opaque.
In a small bowl, mix together soy sauce, sesame oil, honey (or sugar substitute), and rice vinegar to make the sauce.
Pour the sauce over the shrimp and vegetables in the skillet. Stir well to combine.
Cook for another 1-2 minutes, allowing the sauce to thicken slightly and coat the shrimp and vegetables.
Once everything is heated through and well combined, remove the skillet from the heat.
Garnish with thinly sliced green onions and sesame seeds, if desired.
Serve hot as a delicious and flavorful Korean-style stir-fried shrimp and vegetables.
Enjoy your tasty and nutritious dish!

Low-Carb Kimchi Fried Cauliflower Rice

Ingredients:

- 1 medium head cauliflower
- 1 cup kimchi, chopped
- 2 cloves garlic, minced
- 2 green onions, thinly sliced
- 2 tablespoons soy sauce or tamari
- 1 tablespoon sesame oil
- 1 tablespoon gochujang (Korean chili paste), optional for spice
- 1 tablespoon cooking oil
- Sesame seeds, for garnish (optional)

Instructions:

Cut the cauliflower into florets and place them in a food processor. Pulse until the cauliflower resembles rice grains, or use a box grater to grate the cauliflower into rice-like pieces.

Heat cooking oil in a large skillet or wok over medium-high heat.

Add minced garlic to the skillet. Sauté for about 1 minute until fragrant.

Add chopped kimchi to the skillet. Cook for another 2-3 minutes, stirring occasionally.

Add the cauliflower rice to the skillet. Stir-fry for 4-5 minutes until it is tender but not mushy.

In a small bowl, mix together soy sauce, sesame oil, and gochujang (if using).

Pour the sauce over the cauliflower rice in the skillet. Stir well to combine.

Cook for another 2-3 minutes, allowing the flavors to meld together.

Once everything is heated through and well combined, remove the skillet from the heat.

Garnish with thinly sliced green onions and sesame seeds, if desired.

Serve hot as a delicious and low-carb kimchi fried cauliflower rice.

Enjoy your flavorful and satisfying meal!

Korean-style Spicy Cabbage Salad

Ingredients:

- 4 cups shredded cabbage
- 1 carrot, julienned
- 2 green onions, thinly sliced
- 2 tablespoons Korean red pepper flakes (gochugaru)
- 1 tablespoon soy sauce
- 1 tablespoon rice vinegar
- 1 tablespoon sesame oil
- 1 teaspoon honey or sugar substitute
- 1 clove garlic, minced
- 1 teaspoon grated ginger
- Salt, to taste
- Sesame seeds, for garnish (optional)

Instructions:

In a large bowl, combine shredded cabbage, julienned carrot, and thinly sliced green onions.

In a small bowl, whisk together Korean red pepper flakes, soy sauce, rice vinegar, sesame oil, honey (or sugar substitute), minced garlic, and grated ginger to make the dressing.

Pour the dressing over the cabbage mixture in the large bowl. Toss until everything is evenly coated.

Taste and adjust seasoning with salt if needed.

Cover the bowl and refrigerate for at least 30 minutes to allow the flavors to meld together.

Just before serving, garnish the spicy Korean cabbage salad with sesame seeds, if desired.

Serve chilled as a refreshing and spicy side dish.

Enjoy your delicious Korean-style spicy cabbage salad!

Cauliflower Kimchi Stir-Fry

Ingredients:

- 1 medium head cauliflower
- 1 cup kimchi, chopped
- 2 cloves garlic, minced
- 1 tablespoon sesame oil
- 2 green onions, thinly sliced
- 1 tablespoon soy sauce
- 1 teaspoon honey or sugar substitute
- Sesame seeds, for garnish (optional)

Instructions:

Cut the cauliflower into florets and place them in a food processor. Pulse until the cauliflower resembles rice grains, or use a box grater to grate the cauliflower into rice-like pieces.

Heat sesame oil in a large skillet or wok over medium-high heat.

Add minced garlic to the skillet. Sauté for about 1 minute until fragrant.

Add chopped kimchi to the skillet. Cook for another 2-3 minutes, stirring occasionally.

Add the cauliflower rice to the skillet. Stir-fry for 4-5 minutes until it is tender but not mushy.

In a small bowl, mix together soy sauce and honey (or sugar substitute).

Pour the soy sauce mixture over the cauliflower kimchi mixture in the skillet. Stir well to combine.

Cook for another 2-3 minutes, allowing the flavors to meld together.

Once everything is heated through and well combined, remove the skillet from the heat.

Garnish with thinly sliced green onions and sesame seeds, if desired.

Serve hot as a delicious and flavorful cauliflower kimchi stir-fry.

Enjoy your tasty and nutritious dish!

Korean Beef and Bean Sprout Stir-Fry

Ingredients:

- 1 lb (450g) beef sirloin or flank steak, thinly sliced
- 2 cups bean sprouts
- 1 onion, thinly sliced
- 2 cloves garlic, minced
- 2 tablespoons soy sauce
- 1 tablespoon sesame oil
- 1 tablespoon brown sugar or sugar substitute
- 1 tablespoon rice vinegar
- 2 green onions, thinly sliced (for garnish)
- Cooking oil
- Sesame seeds (for garnish, optional)

Instructions:

Heat a bit of cooking oil in a large skillet or wok over medium-high heat.

Add thinly sliced onion to the skillet. Stir-fry for 2-3 minutes until the onion begins to soften.

Add thinly sliced beef to the skillet. Stir-fry for 4-5 minutes until the beef is browned and cooked through.

Push the cooked beef to one side of the skillet and add the bean sprouts to the other side. Stir-fry for 2-3 minutes until the bean sprouts are just tender.

In a small bowl, mix together soy sauce, sesame oil, brown sugar (or sugar substitute), and rice vinegar to make the sauce.

Pour the sauce over the beef and bean sprouts in the skillet. Stir well to combine.

Cook for another 1-2 minutes, allowing the sauce to thicken slightly and coat the beef and bean sprouts.

Once everything is heated through and well combined, remove the skillet from the heat.

Garnish with thinly sliced green onions and sesame seeds, if desired.

Serve hot as a delicious and flavorful Korean beef and bean sprout stir-fry.

Enjoy your tasty and nutritious dish!

Spicy Korean Chicken and Vegetable Skewers

Ingredients:

- 1 lb (450g) boneless, skinless chicken breasts or thighs, cut into bite-sized pieces
- 2 bell peppers (any color), cut into chunks
- 1 onion, cut into chunks
- 1 zucchini, sliced into rounds
- For the Marinade:
    - 3 tablespoons gochujang (Korean chili paste)
    - 2 tablespoons soy sauce
    - 1 tablespoon sesame oil
    - 1 tablespoon honey or sugar substitute
    - 2 cloves garlic, minced
    - 1 teaspoon ginger, minced
    - 1 tablespoon rice vinegar
- Skewers, soaked in water if wooden

Instructions:

In a bowl, mix together gochujang, soy sauce, sesame oil, honey (or sugar substitute), minced garlic, minced ginger, and rice vinegar to make the marinade.

Add the chicken pieces to the marinade. Toss until well coated and let it marinate for about 30 minutes in the refrigerator.

Preheat your grill or grill pan to medium-high heat.

Thread the marinated chicken, bell peppers, onion chunks, and zucchini slices onto skewers, alternating between chicken and vegetables.

Place the skewers on the preheated grill. Cook for 5-7 minutes on each side, or until the chicken is cooked through and the vegetables are tender and slightly charred.

While grilling, you can brush the skewers with any remaining marinade for extra flavor.

Once the skewers are cooked, remove them from the grill and transfer them to a serving platter.

Serve hot as a delicious and spicy Korean chicken and vegetable skewers.

Enjoy your flavorful and satisfying meal!

Korean-style Sesame Spinach Salad

Ingredients:

- 1 lb (450g) fresh spinach, washed and trimmed
- 2 tablespoons soy sauce
- 1 tablespoon sesame oil
- 1 tablespoon rice vinegar
- 1 tablespoon honey or sugar substitute
- 2 cloves garlic, minced
- 1 teaspoon grated ginger
- 1 tablespoon sesame seeds
- Salt, to taste

Instructions:

Bring a large pot of water to a boil. Add the spinach and blanch for about 1 minute until wilted.

Drain the spinach and rinse under cold water to stop the cooking process.

Squeeze out excess water and chop the spinach into bite-sized pieces.

In a small bowl, whisk together soy sauce, sesame oil, rice vinegar, honey (or sugar substitute), minced garlic, and grated ginger to make the dressing.

Place the chopped spinach in a large bowl and pour the dressing over it. Toss until well coated.

Taste and adjust seasoning with salt if needed.

Transfer the spinach salad to a serving dish and sprinkle sesame seeds over the top.

Serve chilled as a delicious and flavorful Korean-style sesame spinach salad.

Enjoy your nutritious and refreshing salad!

Low-Carb Kimchi Cauliflower Rice Bowls

Ingredients:

For the Cauliflower Rice:

- 1 medium head cauliflower
- 1 tablespoon sesame oil
- 2 cloves garlic, minced
- 1 cup kimchi, chopped
- 2 tablespoons soy sauce or tamari
- 1 tablespoon rice vinegar
- 1 teaspoon honey or sugar substitute
- Salt, to taste

For Toppings (Optional):

- Cooked protein of choice (such as grilled chicken, tofu, or shrimp)
- Sliced avocado
- Sliced cucumber
- Sesame seeds
- Thinly sliced green onions

Instructions:

Cut the cauliflower into florets and place them in a food processor. Pulse until the cauliflower resembles rice grains, or use a box grater to grate the cauliflower into rice-like pieces.

Heat sesame oil in a large skillet or wok over medium-high heat.

Add minced garlic to the skillet. Sauté for about 1 minute until fragrant.

Add chopped kimchi to the skillet. Cook for another 2-3 minutes, stirring occasionally.

Add the cauliflower rice to the skillet. Stir-fry for 4-5 minutes until it is tender but not mushy.

In a small bowl, mix together soy sauce, rice vinegar, and honey (or sugar substitute).

Pour the soy sauce mixture over the cauliflower rice in the skillet. Stir well to combine.

Cook for another 2-3 minutes, allowing the flavors to meld together. Taste and adjust seasoning with salt if needed.

Once everything is heated through and well combined, remove the skillet from the heat.

Divide the kimchi cauliflower rice into bowls. Top with your choice of cooked protein (if using), sliced avocado, sliced cucumber, sesame seeds, and thinly sliced green onions.

Serve hot or at room temperature as low-carb kimchi cauliflower rice bowls. Enjoy your delicious and satisfying meal!

Spicy Korean Tofu and Mushroom Stir-Fry

Ingredients:

- 1 block (14 oz) firm tofu, cut into cubes
- 2 cups mushrooms (such as shiitake, cremini, or button), sliced
- 2 tablespoons gochujang (Korean chili paste)
- 2 tablespoons soy sauce or tamari
- 1 tablespoon sesame oil
- 1 tablespoon rice vinegar
- 1 tablespoon honey or sugar substitute
- 2 cloves garlic, minced
- 1 teaspoon grated ginger
- 2 green onions, thinly sliced (for garnish)
- 1 tablespoon cooking oil
- Sesame seeds, for garnish (optional)

Instructions:

In a small bowl, mix together gochujang, soy sauce, sesame oil, rice vinegar, honey (or sugar substitute), minced garlic, and grated ginger to make the sauce.
Heat cooking oil in a large skillet or wok over medium-high heat.
Add cubed tofu to the skillet. Stir-fry for 4-5 minutes until lightly browned on all sides.
Add sliced mushrooms to the skillet. Stir-fry for another 3-4 minutes until the mushrooms are tender.
Pour the sauce over the tofu and mushrooms in the skillet. Stir well to combine.
Cook for another 2-3 minutes, allowing the sauce to coat the tofu and mushrooms and thicken slightly.
Once everything is heated through and well combined, remove the skillet from the heat.
Garnish with thinly sliced green onions and sesame seeds, if desired.
Serve hot as a delicious and spicy Korean tofu and mushroom stir-fry.
Enjoy your flavorful and satisfying meal!

Korean Beef and Bell Pepper Stir-Fry

Ingredients:

- 1 lb (450g) beef sirloin or flank steak, thinly sliced
- 2 bell peppers (any color), sliced
- 1 onion, sliced
- 2 cloves garlic, minced
- 2 tablespoons soy sauce
- 1 tablespoon sesame oil
- 1 tablespoon brown sugar or sugar substitute
- 1 tablespoon rice vinegar
- 1 tablespoon gochujang (Korean chili paste), optional for spice
- Cooking oil
- Sesame seeds, for garnish (optional)
- Thinly sliced green onions, for garnish (optional)

Instructions:

In a bowl, mix together soy sauce, sesame oil, brown sugar (or sugar substitute), rice vinegar, and gochujang (if using) to make the marinade.

Add thinly sliced beef to the marinade. Toss until well coated and let it marinate for about 15-20 minutes.

Heat a bit of cooking oil in a large skillet or wok over medium-high heat.

Add minced garlic to the skillet. Sauté for about 1 minute until fragrant.

Add sliced bell peppers and onions to the skillet. Stir-fry for 3-4 minutes until they begin to soften.

Push the vegetables to one side of the skillet and add the marinated beef to the other side. Stir-fry for 4-5 minutes until the beef is browned and cooked through.

Once the beef is cooked, combine it with the vegetables in the skillet.

Cook for another 1-2 minutes, allowing the flavors to meld together.

Once everything is heated through and well combined, remove the skillet from the heat.

Garnish with sesame seeds and thinly sliced green onions, if desired.

Serve hot as a delicious and flavorful Korean beef and bell pepper stir-fry.

Enjoy your tasty and nutritious dish!

Kimchi Cauliflower "Fried Rice" Bowls

Ingredients:

For the Cauliflower Rice:

- 1 medium head cauliflower
- 1 cup kimchi, chopped
- 2 cloves garlic, minced
- 2 green onions, thinly sliced
- 2 tablespoons soy sauce or tamari
- 1 tablespoon sesame oil
- 1 tablespoon gochujang (Korean chili paste), optional for spice
- 1 tablespoon cooking oil
- Sesame seeds, for garnish (optional)

For Toppings (Optional):

- Fried or scrambled eggs
- Cooked protein of choice (such as grilled chicken, tofu, or shrimp)
- Sliced avocado
- Sliced cucumber
- Thinly sliced green onions

Instructions:

Cut the cauliflower into florets and place them in a food processor. Pulse until the cauliflower resembles rice grains, or use a box grater to grate the cauliflower into rice-like pieces.

Heat cooking oil in a large skillet or wok over medium-high heat.

Add minced garlic to the skillet. Sauté for about 1 minute until fragrant.

Add chopped kimchi to the skillet. Cook for another 2-3 minutes, stirring occasionally.

Add the cauliflower rice to the skillet. Stir-fry for 4-5 minutes until it is tender but not mushy.

In a small bowl, mix together soy sauce, sesame oil, and gochujang (if using).

Pour the soy sauce mixture over the cauliflower rice in the skillet. Stir well to combine.

Cook for another 2-3 minutes, allowing the flavors to meld together.

Once everything is heated through and well combined, remove the skillet from the heat.

Divide the kimchi cauliflower rice into bowls. Top with fried or scrambled eggs, cooked protein (if using), sliced avocado, sliced cucumber, and thinly sliced green onions.
Garnish with sesame seeds, if desired.
Serve hot as a delicious and flavorful kimchi cauliflower "fried rice" bowl.
Enjoy your tasty and nutritious meal!

Korean-style Spicy Zucchini Noodles

Ingredients:

- 4 medium zucchini
- 2 tablespoons soy sauce or tamari
- 1 tablespoon sesame oil
- 1 tablespoon gochujang (Korean chili paste)
- 1 tablespoon rice vinegar
- 1 tablespoon honey or sugar substitute
- 2 cloves garlic, minced
- 1 teaspoon grated ginger
- 2 green onions, thinly sliced (for garnish)
- 1 tablespoon cooking oil
- Sesame seeds, for garnish (optional)

Instructions:

Trim the ends of the zucchini and spiralize them into noodles using a spiralizer. Alternatively, you can use a julienne peeler to create zucchini noodles.
In a small bowl, whisk together soy sauce, sesame oil, gochujang, rice vinegar, honey (or sugar substitute), minced garlic, and grated ginger to make the sauce.
Heat cooking oil in a large skillet or wok over medium-high heat.
Add the zucchini noodles to the skillet. Stir-fry for 2-3 minutes until they begin to soften.
Pour the sauce over the zucchini noodles in the skillet. Stir well to combine.
Cook for another 2-3 minutes, allowing the noodles to absorb the flavors of the sauce.
Once the noodles are cooked to your desired consistency and coated in the sauce, remove the skillet from the heat.
Divide the spicy zucchini noodles into serving bowls.
Garnish with thinly sliced green onions and sesame seeds, if desired.
Serve hot as a delicious and spicy Korean-style zucchini noodles.
Enjoy your flavorful and satisfying low-carb meal!